RUTH
BADER
GINSBURG

By Jonah Winter

Illustrated by Stacy Innerst

★ THE CASE of R. B. G. vs. INEQUALITY ★

ABRAMS BOOKS *for* YOUNG READERS

NEW YORK

Ladies and gentlemen of the jury: During this trial, you will learn about a little girl who had no clue just how important she would become. You will see the unfair world she was born into—where boys were valued more than girls, where women were not encouraged to achieve and aspire. You will see evidence of that unfairness, just as she herself has seen it all her life.

Here are the facts of her case.

Ruth Bader was born on March 15, 1933—the daughter of two Jewish parents whose families had fled Europe for Brooklyn, New York, to escape anti-Jewish persecution.

Her father owned a fur shop for many years. When the shop went out of business, he got a job at a clothing store. He was uneducated—he had never finished high school.

Ruth's mother graduated from high school at the age of fifteen, smart enough that she might have gone to college. But at this point in history, girls were discouraged from going to college. So Ruth's mother got a job to help pay for her *brother's* college education. Next came marriage—and a husband who discouraged her from working outside the home. Like many men of his time, he thought that "a woman's place was in the home." This was what Ruth saw as a girl.

What Ruth also saw was a mother who loved books and loved to read—and a mother who wanted her daughter to have the good education that she herself had been denied. Ruth saw a mother who saved every penny she could for her daughter to someday go to college.

Once a week, Ruth's mother dropped her off at the local library, which was above a Chinese restaurant, and left her there while she was getting her hair done.

Surrounded by books and the smell of Chinese food, Ruth
would choose three books to take home for the week. She liked
books about mythology—and Nancy Drew mysteries.

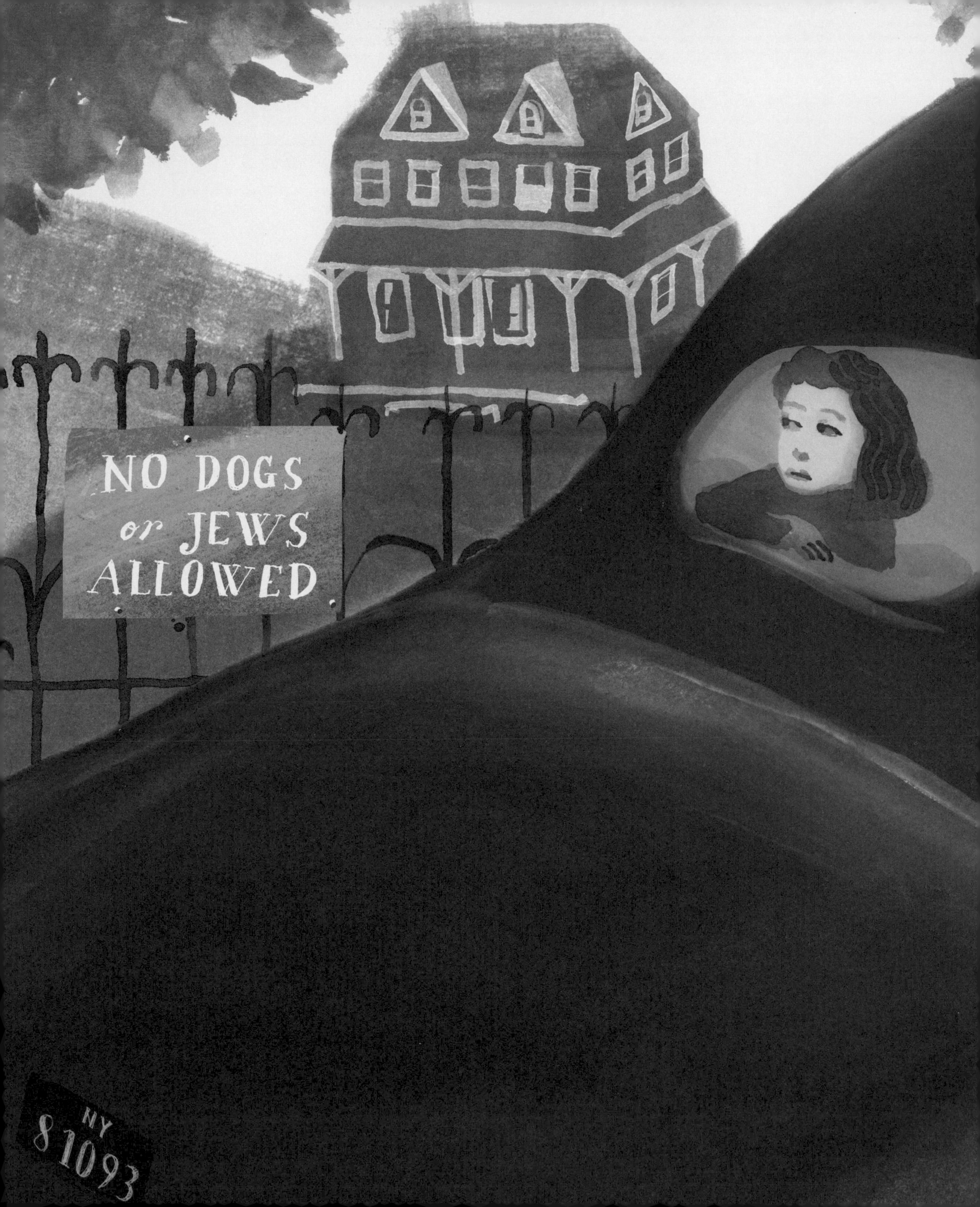
NO DOGS
or JEWS
ALLOWED
NY
81093

This all happened in Brooklyn, which has long been home to lots of Jewish families and businesses. Brooklyn has also been home to anti-Jewish violence and vandalism. During the 1930s and 1940s, to be Jewish in America was to know anti-Semitism.

We now offer into evidence: Anti-Semitism experienced firsthand by Ruth—a sign outside a resort in Pennsylvania, seen from her parents' car. It said: NO DOGS OR JEWS ALLOWED. This happened right here in America.

Being smart can be a great defense against such meanness and stupidity—and Ruth was one smart cookie. She tied for highest grades in her elementary school, where she wrote an essay about the Magna Carta and the Bill of Rights called "Landmarks of Constitutional Freedom"—evidence of an early interest in law, in justice, in words.

This is not to say she always knew what she wanted to be. In high school, Ruth had many interests and hobbies—editing the school newspaper, playing cello in the orchestra, and even twirling a baton at football games (and once chipping a tooth in the process).

The day on which Ruth would graduate from high school, with honors,
promised to be a glorious day. She ranked sixth out of a class of 700,
and she had won a New York State scholarship for college. But Ruth was
nowhere to be seen at the ceremony.

That's because she stayed home. Ruth's mother had been ill with cancer for four years. And on the very day Ruth was to graduate, her mother died. Instead of wearing a cap and gown and being honored, Ruth was mourning the death of the person she loved most in the world, the person whose dream was to see Ruth go on to college . . . and become an independent woman.

There was only one thing for Ruth to do. Suitcase in hand, she arrived at Cornell University—the same university her mother's brother had gone to, the same university her mother might have gone to, had she been encouraged.

It was 1950, and very few girls went to college. At Cornell, male students outnumbered female students four to one. For a girl to get into Cornell, she had to be very smart. But she had to pretend *not* to be smart if she wanted a boy to ask her out on a date. She could not be seen studying.

This was a problem for Ruth, who was a very serious student. Her solution was to do her studying in the bathroom, where no boys would see her. That's just how things were.

And then along came Martin Ginsburg. Martin was different from any boy she'd ever met—he liked that she had a brain. And Ruth was different from any girl he'd met. She had dreams of having a career, of being independent. She spoke only when she had something interesting to say. And she was always listening, always thinking, always learning.

In her constitutional law class, Ruth learned about freedom of speech and freedom of the press—freedoms all Americans are guaranteed in the Constitution. She learned about a senator named Joseph McCarthy, who was trying to take away these important rights—and brave lawyers who were fighting him in court. Learning about these lawyers made Ruth want to become one. She believed she could be a good lawyer—and support herself.

But the decision to become a lawyer was not an easy one for a woman to make in 1954. There were very few female lawyers in America. Ruth's own father discouraged her from going to law school, because he believed she wouldn't get a job. Besides, *her place was in the home.*

Ruth refused to listen to her father. She saw no reason why she should not become a lawyer. She was just as smart and capable as any man. Her verdict was final—she would go to law school. But first, she would get married—to her first and only love, Martin Ginsburg.

And now, girls and boys of the jury, we offer into evidence some of the more outrageous nonsense Ruth endured—before, during, and after law school.

Exhibit A: It was her first job out of college, right before law school. Her boss demoted her and slashed her wages— because he saw she was pregnant. This was a common practice.

What could Ruth do?

B.

MEN'S RESIDENCE

Exhibit B: Arrival at Harvard Law School, where there were only nine women in a class of 500. Harvard did not even provide a place for the women to live. Not very welcoming!

C.

Exhibit C: In the law library, she was barred from entering the periodical room because she was a woman. The guard would not let her in—nor help her in any way. She needed a book from this room. How was she supposed to complete her assignment?

Exhibit D: Most classes had just one woman per class. For comic relief, the professor in the lecture hall would often call on the lone woman, such as Ruth, as if it were a joke. But the woman almost always answered correctly. She had to. She was representing all women.

Exhibit E: One night, the law school dean invited all nine female students, including Ruth, to a dinner at his house. He sat each woman next to a male law professor. He then went around the table, asking each female student why she thought she deserved a spot in this law school that could have gone to a man. Ruth's answer: "To better understand the work of my husband."

And yet, without Ruth's help, her husband—who was also a student at Harvard Law School—would not have graduated. He became gravely ill and was unable to attend classes. Ruth went to his classes for him and took notes, so that he could pass his courses. She also took care of him, took care of their newborn baby, Jane, went to her *own* classes, *and* was an editor of the *Harvard Law Review*.

Martin recovered, graduated, and got a job at a law firm in New York City. So Ruth transferred from Harvard Law School to New York's Columbia Law School—and tied for *first in class* when she graduated. Surely, Ruth would get a job, right? But at Columbia's job placement center, most job postings said "men only."

Exhibit F: Even among the law firms supposedly open to hiring women, not one firm would hire her. She was a woman, she was Jewish, AND she was a mother.

Ruth just shrugged and moved on—first to a job as a law clerk, then as a law professor—only to encounter unfairness again and again.

Exhibit G: At Rutgers University, she found out that female professors were being paid less than male professors. She and another woman sued the school—and won.

Hers   His

G.

H.

Exhibit H: Ruth would speak up at faculty meetings—and the male professors would totally ignore her. A male professor would then say the very same thing that Ruth had said—and get acknowledged for being smart. This kept happening even after Ruth became Columbia's first tenured female law professor.

By the 1970s, a lot of women had had enough of this sort of treatment. They took part in protests and demonstrations with signs saying ENOUGH IS ENOUGH, EQUAL PAY FOR EQUAL JOBS, WOMEN'S LIBERATION, and EQUALITY!

It wasn't Ruth's style to take part in protests, but she did do something. An organization called the American Civil Liberties Union (ACLU) asked Ruth to be in charge of court cases involving women's inequality. The reason they asked her? Because she was a woman, and they thought this was "women's work"! There was no end to this disrespect.

Nonetheless, Ruth accepted the position, and in 1972 she became the leader of the ACLU Women's Rights Project—a battle in the courts against unfairness to women. She was the lead lawyer for six Supreme Court cases, and she won five of them. Though Ruth herself was not a revolutionary, what she did for women was revolutionary. She won the right for women to get "equal protection" of the laws—to be treated as equal to men.

EQUAL PAY

EQUALITY!

EQUAL PAY!

EQUALITY

Enough is Enough!

WOMEN'S LIBERATION

Ruth had become a lawyer not to change the world. She'd become a lawyer because she knew she had the verbal and analytical skills to handle the job as well as any man. But here she was, the most important female lawyer in America, fighting and winning legal battles for all American women. Here she was, changing the world.

That's why, in 1980, she was chosen by President Jimmy Carter to be a judge for the most important court of law in America besides the Supreme Court: the U.S. Court of Appeals. She was only the second woman in history to serve on this court. Now it was her job to make judgments, to judge what was and wasn't legal. A good judge listens closely, chooses words carefully, and values fairness above all else. This job suited Ruth perfectly.

After thirteen years of being a judge, at the age of sixty, Ruth got a phone call one night. It was from President Bill Clinton. He wanted to appoint her to the Supreme Court—to be just the second female Supreme Court Justice in history. As a girl, Ruth never dreamt she would be a lawyer or a judge—much less a Supreme Court Justice.

In her acceptance speech, she spoke of her mother: "I pray that I may be all that she would have been had she lived in an age when women could aspire and achieve, and daughters are cherished as much as sons."

When Ruth arrived on the Court, the first female Supreme Court Justice—
Sandra Day O'Connor—was still serving. When Sandra retired, Ruth was the
only woman on the Supreme Court for a few years—tiny and outnumbered.
And yet, what she brought to the Court was enormous: dignity, civility,
intelligence, and a soft-spoken manner. She also brought some of the most
powerful, strongly worded dissents in Supreme Court history.

A "dissent" is when a Supreme Court Justice disagrees with the opinion of the majority of the nine judges. In Ruth's case, a dissent often involves a written statement—perfectly worded—that rips apart the opinion of the majority.

Physical toughness is another of Ruth's trademarks. In 2009, she found out she had cancer and needed surgery. Only nineteen days after her operation, she returned to the Court. She did so because she wanted people—especially young women—to see at least one woman on the Supreme Court.

At any number of points in her life, Ruth could have given up. She could have listened to her father. She could have dropped out of law school. She could have abandoned her search for a job. She could have accepted being paid less than her male associates. Instead, she stayed on the difficult path she chose for herself, removing one obstacle after the next—until she arrived at the very court that is the symbol of justice in America.

There can be just one verdict: Because she did not give up, because she refused to let other people define her limitations as a person, Ruth Bader Ginsburg has herself become a symbol of justice in America.

Men Only

NO DOGS or JEWS ALLOWED

GLOSSARY

AMENDMENT: As it applies to the U.S. Constitution, an amendment is an alteration or addition made to the original Constitution. Amendments are generated by Congress and must be approved by a majority (at least three-fourths) of the states in order to become ratified as law.

AMERICAN CIVIL LIBERTIES UNION (ACLU): An organization that defends Americans' basic rights by filing lawsuits in local, state, and federal courts and by lobbying local, state, and federal lawmakers to pass laws that defend civil liberties.

ANTI-SEMITISM: Prejudice, discrimination, vandalism, and/or violence against people who are Jewish.

APPEAL: A formal legal challenge to a court's decision, filed with a higher court.

BILL OF RIGHTS: The first ten amendments to the U.S. Constitution, outlining the basic rights of American citizens, such as freedom of speech and freedom of the press.

CIVIL LAW: Laws pertaining to individual rights and remedies for infringements of those rights. In a civil lawsuit, a plaintiff files a complaint against a defendant for a perceived injury or loss. Judges or juries may award the plaintiff "damages" (money), if the plaintiff wins, to be paid to the plaintiff by the defendant. Or in the case of a constitutional rights case, the court may enforce a remedy to the problem brought to the court's attention by the plaintiff. For instance, in the case of *Loving v. Virginia* (1967), the Supreme Court ruled that the state of Virginia had no right to prohibit interracial marriage.

COLUMBIA LAW SCHOOL: A graduate school within Columbia, a prestigious Ivy League university, located in New York City, and one of the best law schools in America.

CORNELL UNIVERSITY: A prestigious Ivy League university located in Upstate New York.

COURT OF LAW: Refers to (a) the room in which a trial takes place and (b) the institution through which legal matters are settled.

CRIMINAL LAW: Laws pertaining to crime, prosecuted by the government against individuals accused of crimes. Guilt or innocence may be decided by juries or judges. When guilt is determined, penalties may involve imprisonment and/or fines.

DEFENDANT: In a criminal case: the individual who stands charged of a crime by the government. In a civil case: the party (individual, business, or government agency) being sued for wrongdoing by another party.

DISSENT: In the context of a Supreme Court case, a Supreme Court Justice's argument written in response to the Court's majority opinion. It can spell out the argument for a future Supreme Court decision—and can serve the purpose of protesting an unfair law. In one dissent (*Ledbetter v. Goodyear Tire & Rubber Co.*), Justice Ginsburg wrote that Congress should change a particular law, and she read her strong dissent aloud. Soon thereafter, Congress responded to her challenge with the Lilly Ledbetter Fair Pay Act of 2009, which gives employees more rights to challenge wage discrimination through lawsuits.

EQUAL PROTECTION CLAUSE: The part of the U.S. Constitution, in the Fourteenth Amendment, that prohibits states from denying any person "equal protection of the laws."

EVIDENCE: Objects, documents, and facts used in a court of law to back up a legal argument.

EXHIBIT: The legal name for a piece of evidence that is presented in court.

FREEDOM OF SPEECH: A civil right, protected in the First Amendment to the U.S. Constitution, guaranteeing the right of American citizens to say or write anything they wish to say or write without legal penalty. However, there are limitations to this freedom, such as speech that incites people to violence. The Supreme Court has the ultimate power to decide what speech is, and isn't, protected by the First Amendment.

FREEDOM OF THE PRESS: Another civil right protected in the First Amendment to the U.S. Constitution, ensuring citizens' right to publish any piece of writing without legal penalty. However, there are limitations to this freedom, such as in instances of libel, which is the publication of a false statement that damages a person's or a business's reputation. The Supreme Court has the ultimate power to decide disputes concerning this freedom.

HARVARD LAW REVIEW: The most important law school journal in America, edited and published by students of Harvard Law School, containing essays on legal matters.

HARVARD LAW SCHOOL: The most prestigious law school in America—and part of the most prestigious Ivy League university in America, located in Cambridge, Massachusetts.

JOSEPH McCARTHY: A U.S. senator from Wisconsin, who during the early 1950s accused various people in the U.S. government of being traitors and communists, most spectacularly in a Senate hearing in 1954, during which he accused the U.S. Army of harboring communists, prompting the famous quote from the Army's chief counsel, Joseph Welch: "Have you no sense of decency, sir?" McCarthy's public humiliation of those whose opinions he disagreed with had the effect of denying them their constitutional right to free speech (and, in certain cases, ruining their careers and lives).

JUDGE: A government official who presides over a court of law—in some cases acting as the overseer of a jury whose job is to make a decision, and in other cases being the one (or one of a panel) to make that decision.

LAWSUIT: Specific to civil law, a complaint filed by a party (individual, group, company, or government agency) against another party.

LAWYER: Someone who is licensed to practice law in any number of capacities: defending a client in a criminal case, prosecuting a defendant in a criminal case, representing a plaintiff in a civil case, representing a defendant in a civil case, providing legal advice, or representing a corporation.

MAGNA CARTA: Perhaps the most famous legal document in the world, created in 1215 in England, outlining the basic democratic rights of English citizens and establishing "the rule of law," the important principle that laws apply to everybody.

PLAINTIFF: In a civil case, the party (an individual, a group, a company, or a government agency) that brings a lawsuit against another party.

SUPREME COURT: The highest court of law in the United States, whose function is to interpret the laws set forth in the U.S. Constitution, interpret the power of those laws in relation to the laws of the individual states, and decide important lawsuits. In so doing, the Supreme Court sets legal precedent for all the lower courts throughout America— determining what is and is not legal. Decisions are made by a majority of the nine justices in any given case.

SUPREME COURT JUSTICE: The term used to describe any of the nine members of the Supreme Court—the highest-ranking judges in America.

U.S. CONGRESS: The House of Representatives and the Senate—the two groups of elected lawmakers who, along with the president, govern the United States, creating new laws and deciding on issues that affect all Americans, such as taxes and declarations of war. Their meeting halls are in the U.S. Capitol Building in Washington, D.C., the capital of America.

U.S. CONSTITUTION: America's original rule book, ratified in 1788. It laid down the laws that apply to the entire country, establishing everything from how America's government works to the rights of all American citizens.

U.S. COURT OF APPEALS: The second highest court in America (after the Supreme Court), to which individuals who are unhappy with a lower court's decision may "appeal" for a different decision.

WOMEN'S LIBERATION MOVEMENT: A political movement during the 1960s and 1970s through which many women organized to demand equal rights for women under the law and to protest various forms of discrimination toward women.

WOMEN'S RIGHTS PROJECT: A series of lawsuits filed by the ACLU between 1971 and 1976, led by Ruth Bader Ginsburg, addressing and seeking to remedy various ways in which women were not equal to men before the law. The first case, *Reed v. Reed*, led to a groundbreaking decision by the Supreme Court, which, by means of the Equal Protection Clause of the Constitution, ensured equal protection for men and women under the law in the administration of estates. Altogether, the Supreme Court cases won by the Women's Rights Project amounted to significant progress in the legal equality of women and men in America.

AUTHOR'S NOTE

RUTH JOAN BADER GINSBURG WAS BORN IN BROOKLYN, New York, on March 15, 1933. She became a lawyer not to promote women's rights but simply because she thought she "could do a lawyer's job better than any other." Reserved and conservative by nature, she was not originally what you'd call a maverick. But the obstacles she encountered as a woman pursuing a career path in an unjust, male-dominated field and society turned her into one. During her law school years, she was the first woman ever on both the *Harvard Law Review* and the *Columbia Law Review*. In 1972, after successfully suing Rutgers University for discrimination against women, she became Columbia University Law School's first tenured female law professor. That same year, she was appointed cofounder and director of the ACLU's Women's Rights Project, becoming one of the most prominent promoters of women's rights of the 1970s—an era of women's rights advancements for which she was in large part responsible. During her years with the ACLU, she furthered the notion of "equal protection" for women and men under the law (as defined in the 14th Amendment of the U.S. Constitution)—and participated in 34 Supreme Court cases, winning five of the six cases that she herself argued before the Supreme Court as lead or co-counsel. In each of the 34 cases she oversaw, she used the logic that inequality between men and women hurts both men and women. She fought against stereotyping men *or* women because of their gender. In certain cases, she defended a man's right not be stereotyped or denied certain rights or privileges due to his gender. It was a brilliant way of promoting the cause of equal rights.

After her groundbreaking work as a lawyer came her appointment to the U.S. Court of Appeals in 1980; she was one of a record-breaking 40 female appointments to the federal bench made by President Jimmy Carter. When he took office in 1977, there was only one female federal judge (out of 97) in America; out of 399 District Court judges, only five were female. In 1993, Ruth became the first Jewish woman and only the second woman in history to be appointed as a Justice to the Supreme Court, where she is still serving as of the publication of this book. As a Supreme Court Justice, she has distinguished herself through strongly worded dissents—most notably in the cases *Bush v. Gore* (2000), *Shelby County v. Holder* (2013), and *Burwell v. Hobby Lobby* (2014). And she has made her mark as the most politically liberal member of the Court in many regards. Through her votes as a Justice, she has continued her advocacy for women's rights, and she has also voted in favor of voting rights for African Americans, affirmative action to help combat discrimination against African American students, criminal background checks for people who want to buy guns, and the right for gay couples to marry. Her opposition to the *Citizens United v. FEC* decision, by which a majority of the Supreme Court determined that corporations are people (and therefore are privileged to the right of "free speech" and the right to spend an unlimited amount of money on swaying elections), is famous. (She has called it the "most disappointing" Supreme Court decision during her time on the Court.)

Her reputation as a firebrand has inspired a younger generation of equal rights and social justice advocates—enough so that she has become a bit of a rock star, her image emblazoned on T-shirts with the words "Notorious R.B.G," a reference to hip-hop artist Notorious B.I.G. Ruth loves every minute of it! And so do her granddaughters! At age 84, R.B.G. shows no signs of slowing down. She still does her Canadian Air Force exercise workout every day. And she still writes her written responses to every case at a faster rate than any of her younger colleagues. When asked how many women on the Supreme Court would "be enough," she responds: "When there are nine." YES!

For my godson,
Rhys Malcolm Black.

—J.W.

For Susan Cohen.

—S.I.

The illustrations in this book were made with gouache, ink, and Photoshop.

Library of Congress Cataloging-in-Publication Data
Names: Winter, Jonah, 1962– author. | Innerst, Stacy, illustrator.
Title: Ruth Bader Ginsburg: the case of R. B. G. vs. inequality / by
    Jonah Winter ; illustrated by Stacy Innerst.
Description: New York : Abrams Books for Young Readers, [2018]
Identifiers: LCCN 2016042352 | ISBN 9781419725593
Subjects: LCSH: Ginsburg, Ruth Bader—Juvenile literature. | Women
    judges—United States—Biography—Juvenile literature. | Jewish
    judges—United States—Biography—Juvenile literature. | Judges—United
    States—Biography—Juvenile literature. | United States. Supreme
    Court—Biography—Juvenile literature.
Classification: LCC KF8745.G56 W56 2018 | DDC 347.73/2634 [B] —dc23
LC record available at https://lccn.loc.gov/2016042352

Text copyright © 2017 Jonah Winter
Illustrations copyright © 2017 Stacy Innerst
Book design by Pamela Notarantonio

Printed and bound in China
10 9 8 7 6 5 4 3 2 1

Abrams Books for Young Readers are available at special discounts when
purchased in quantity for premiums and promotions as well as fundraising
or educational use. Special editions can also be created to specification.
For details, contact specialsales@abramsbooks.com or the address below.

ABRAMS The Art of Books
115 West 18th Street, New York, NY 10011
abramsbooks.com